Manoleria

Tupelo Press / *Crazyhorse* **Book Award**
Previously the Tupelo Press First Book Award

Jennifer Michael Hecht, *The Last Ancient World*
Selected by Janet Holmes

Aimee Nezhukumatathil, *Miracle Fruit*
Selected by Gregory Orr

Bill Van Every, *Devoted Creatures*
Selected by Thomas Lux

David Petruzelli, *Everyone Coming Toward You*
Selected by Campbell McGrath

Lillias Bever, *Bellini in Istanbul*
Selected by Michael Collier

Dwaine Rieves, *When the Eye Forms*
Selected by Carolyn Forché

Kristin Bock, *Cloisters*
Selected by David St. John

Jennifer Militello, *Flinch of Song*
Megan Snyder–Camp, *The Forest of Sure Things*
Daniel Khalastchi, *Manoleria*
Selected by Carol Ann Davis, Garrett Doherty, and Jeffrey Levine

Manoleria

Poems

Daniel Khalastchi

T|P

Tupelo Press
North Adams, Massachusetts

Manoleria
Copyright 2011 Daniel Khalastchi. All rights reserved.

Library of Congress Cataloging–in–Publication Data

Khalastchi, Daniel, 1980–
    Manoleria : poems / Daniel Khalastchi. — 1st pbk. ed.
        p. cm. — (Tupelo Press/Crazyhorse First Book Award)
    ISBN 978–1–932195–93–4 (pbk. : alk. paper)
    I. Title.
    PS3611.H33M36 2011
    811'.6—dc22
                                2010047364

Cover and text designed by William Kuch, WK Design.
Cover: "Pose" (2006), painting by Tala Madani. Used with permission of the
artist (see her work at The Saatchi Gallery online: http://www.saatchi–gallery.
co.uk/artists/tala_madani.htm)

First paperback edition: February 2011.
15 14 13 12 11   5 4 3 2 1

Printed in the United States.

Other than brief excerpts for reviews and commentaries, no part of this book
may be reproduced by any means without permission of the publisher. Please
address requests for reprint permission or for course–adoption discounts to:

Tupelo Press
P.O. Box 1767
243 Union Street, Eclipse Mill, Loft 305
North Adams, Massachusetts 01247
Telephone: (413) 664–9611 / Fax: (413) 664–9711
editor@tupelopress.org / www.tupelopress.org

Tupelo Press is an award–winning independent literary press that publishes
fine fiction, non–fiction, and poetry in books that are a joy to hold as well as
read. Tupelo Press is a registered 501(c)3 non–profit organization, and we
rely on public support to carry out our mission of publishing extraordinary
work that may be outside the realm of large commercial publishers. Financial
donations are welcome and are tax deductible.

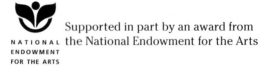

Supported in part by an award from
NATIONAL the National Endowment for the Arts
ENDOWMENT
FOR THE ARTS

For Caryl

Contents

I:

II:

What do you do to go on.
I do the same.

Gertrude Stein

The Maturation Of Man:

Because   rain. Because hard. Because
pain in my   ribs, because   buckle and
wait. Because   cramping. Because
kneeling   low. Because pause. Because
fact. Because wings   unreel   the flat
spread of my stomach. Because   feathers. Because
damp. Because red,   white,
because loose the skin   falls to all–   pile my
shoes. Because shirt. Because torn. Because
buttons un–   done, because   chest a pale
fire. Because   calm. Because   thinking
through. Because   steady. Because focused. Because
bones   straighten,   retract   in a
fold. Because   movement. Because pushing
out. Because stretch,   because reach,   because weak
the growth spreads like   sick sheets   on a line. Because
quiet. Because   broken   down. Because phone
calls,   mothers, because   children scream
softly they   still want to   touch me.   Because
sirens. Because   cameras and tanks. Because there
is   no choice but   to head   for the hills.   Because
terror. Because   running   scared. Because   breathe, because
breathe, because spasms,   beats.   Because   from a bench I
step   to the air—   watch   as my   city
folds   down   to a circle.

National Growth:

I awake in   the dirt
of a garden. From

pelvis to   neck my
body is covered. When

I breathe, small   pebbles
and   beetles roll low

to a footpath. People
walk   by, taking

pictures of   flowers. If
I stretch I can

reach a thin tin
pail of water. Pour–

ing it over my   sternum I
hear bones   break part in

elegant stress. A
row of haired   carrot

tops sink straight through
my nipples. Their roots

grab for   vessels,
for   spine, and I   bite

my lip while they   steady
their hold. Somewhere a

radio plays soft
news of a shooting. A couple

comes near holding
drinks with umbrellas. I

feel such   weight lay
heavy my stomach. See red

heads of   lettuce where
I was told I have ovaries.

Fear And Greed Index:

We are rushed
from our dinner. Men
with axes tear down

a wall near the kitchen,
and a line is formed out–
side to give names and

brief statements. *What
did you see?* I saw red
dresses on women saw hands

under tables. *What
did you hear?* Two chefs
in a fight. *Were you aware*

*a child was being held
behind the drywall?* Yes. Be–
tween courses I would

go to make phone calls—watch
her fed through cracks
in the baseboards, pushing back

bags of gray
stool and dark
urine. *Why didn't you*

say anything? Who would
believe me? My eyes have
been nested. Robins and

grackles weave wheat to
my lashes and twice
a week I find eggs

in my leg. *In your
leg?* It opens like
a piñata. Always at

noon. I twitch and I
cramp and my tibia
folds with a hinge

to my ankle. When it happens,
teenagers from my apartment
complex wait in the courtyard

with waxed twine and
buckets for a neighbor
to wash off the

sinew. *We're sorry
sir, we thought this was
a costume.*

Went We. Inside. My Colon A Tree:
(Diagnosis)

Went we. Inside. My   colon a tree. Broom heavy with   light. With
heavy cut   leaves left. Standing   the spill of. My levee. My
leaving. My find   young   ulcers. Tall kicking   in. Skirts. Legs
white.   High   stockings stored.   Up   low   were
my. Enzymes. And you.   Curtained the.   Colon. Red   salad
your. Shoulder. So long. So   roll.   So   still we   waited
I. Was dis– eased   clean. Under   my sternum.   Here   was
the. Mandarin.   Orange deep water breath   here.   Was
the   steady fed.   Crate where they   saw through
the   inside of   this. Hot future to get   it. Out. Get it
out. Get. It. Out.

Relative Fortune:

On a pier I wait for
the signal to start
my engine. When
given the nod, I fire

the ignition, keeping
my foot pressed hard
on the brake. Night it
is knocking small rolls

at my mirrors. The tide
has pulled back, and to
the east my headlamps
play sharp on a sand–

bar. All around me people
are working. To cover
the sound of tearing tape
and split fuses, I turn

high the defroster. As the
locks are soldered over, I'm
alerted to a checklist
being held against my windshield. Reading

its contents, I give a thumbs
up to show all is accounted
for: plastic bag, handcuffs
and key, hairdryer plugged

to the female end of an extension
cord. The directions that come
next are all much as expected: lock
right wrist to steering wheel,

swallow key, place bag over
head, take very   short   breaths. The
sweat in my beard holds .
heavy in piles. Reaching across my

body, I fasten the seatbelt and shift
away from neutral. When the trunk
is tapped three times, I'm to punch
quick at the gas. There   is one. There
is two. The game makes me smile.

What's Done:

Three girls in a brothel
take me back to their mistress
and wait. When she asks
what's wrong, I look down
at the floor. One of the girls
I've been told to call China says
I should be refunded. The
mistress slides off her reading
glasses and says someone needs
to tell her what the fuck is going
on. China nudges Lacy. Lacy
gets sick. We all move away
from the puddle she's made and the
third girl, Crystal, says it wasn't their
fault. The mistress is getting fed
up with the stalling and screams
loud while tying her robe. The three
women left are raising and raising and
raising their sound when I put out my hand
and everyone stops. In the skin
of my forearm, small fists push
up at odd intervals. If I turn
my wrists, whole bodies of
babies can be seen in profile. Under
the veins they move and sag and when
they touch, they appear to multiply.
China tells me to take off my shirt
and I do it. She tells me to take off
my pants and my shoes but my socks
should stay on until the mistress is
ready. I stand there naked for some
time: my penis erect from the heat
and perfume; my arms, heavy from
the weight of their keep. Crystal brings

me a chair and the mistress asks for a
brandy. When it arrives, she nods and I
make to take off one sock at a time. I pull
the left one down just past the heel and the mistress
hands me my money. Gray tails have pushed
through my Achilles tendon, thrashing
wildly for sense of location. To calm
them down, I feed ice and cheese crackers to the space be–
tween my toes. Walking is difficult. On my stomach,
I crawl to my clothes and get dressed. The
mistress, my sweet, sends word for a taxi.

O Me O My:

Because cargo. Because
food. Because   coal, because
steel, because   track switch   faulty. Because
signals. Because   training.   Because
late night,   no sleep, because   drinks
at the helm.   Because   headaches. Because
sight. Because I see   through seat–
back, through   body, through   seatback, through
body, through wall, through
metal, through   door to large   cliff. Because
panic. Because   screaming.   Because   I see
it coming three   miles away.   Because
teeth. Because   belt. Because belt becomes
rope, becomes   wire cable with
anchor.   Because   window. Because
swing. Because   toss at a   rate, because
tendons   in use. Because   bridge. Because
catch. Because grinding   slow   because
slow   because   slow   because
wait.   Because   needed to. Because
gnawing of corners. Because   spreading and
lift. Because   I take the roof
from my car   to the diner. Make
spoons.   Because   we start digging my
back for a cape. Because under   the branches
they tell me   we find it.

A Series Of Movements:

And with each step tile
lays out before me. It

pushes from the grass
clean without streaks. When

I change my path, the tile
keeps ahead. I walk it

over traps. Through the court–
yard. Around puddles and

manholes, straight into the
ocean where the water grabs

deep for the buoy line. After
every small movement, my

toes reel against the dry, caulk–
colored flooring. I stand still as

possible for what feels like many
minutes: terns and wrens picking

my side for red clams, the tide washing beach
up hard to my knees. Bent back from the

waist, the birds
fill me with shells until

my throat won't close. I cough like
a night bell of Spanish maracas. A hall to dark

sea stays waiting below. My fingers are
boneless. I can't scratch my neck.

By A Fallen Tree I Wait For My Salesman:

He has water
in a pail. Carries it
on a stick
laid over his
shoulder, a net
of old batteries

at the other end
for balance. Coming
upon me he whistles
and coughs. If
the tar and spoiled
meat are a bother, he

doesn't let on. I wrestle
myself free from
the rope, toss it
in the brush just
ahead of the bank. My
chest and neck and

palms are still
numb. Small red–
silvered hooks have been
wrung through my
skin, and socks of
cut animal pull

at their curves. As
the salesman draws closer, I
tuck what I can in the
mess of my back. *Either they
tied bad knots, or you
were too heavy for the*

limb. They cut it
down when I wouldn't
struggle. *Left you
for the wolves?* I show him
my hands. The water swells
up as he sets down his pack. With

his stick, he corrects
my posture—scrapes the sweat
away from my
hairline, comes to me
close with a rag and
an apple. Our legs

are touching. He asks me
to bite on the cotton. Chewing
my shoulder, he feeds back
the apple to the branch to the tree
to the earth.

Manoleria:

Once we reach our cruising altitude, the steward hands me pretzels and a letter from the captain. Since the flight is not full, it asks if I'd mind a few stops en-route to my final destination. It also says not to look down. I do   look down and notice there is no floor beneath me. Around my waist is a belt with my name and last known address branded in the leather; around my neck, a garbage bag and string. When the fasten seatbelt sign is turned back   on, I shake loose a shoe to the influx of air. In my chair, reclined with a blanket, I focus the reading lamp to the sounds of my stomach.

Set Rough Your. Hold My. Ribs Stayed Calm:
(Surgery)

Set rough your. Hold my. Ribs stayed   calm. In.   Open cream
the.   Bandage   ready the.   Damp   crane. Of your. Neck
watched me. Wash.   Down the   water. With   rocks
my   stomach. Treading my.   Stomach walls   settled then
you were. Here   by me we. Counted to   the. Threes of. Our know—
ledge. Once. You cracked the.   Blood was.   Still talking
the.   Lines of its. Measure I.   Heard you   fall to my. Body
was music.

Actual Draw Weight:

I:

For a minute I rest against a
tree drinking water. It is hard
to navigate the forest at night,
but this, I am told, is how it
must be. I have been walking
since morning. My shoes
have been lost. My socks,
torn. My feet are heavy with
sand and clipped bird beaks,
and as I stand to continue the
trail, my bowels are loosed
and I shake to a rhythm. Al–
though it is difficult, I try not
to look at the arrow in my
stomach, or the rope at its
end that is pulled when I
faint. Studded with feathers,
the aluminum shaft burns soft
near my kidneys. Taking no
breaths, we carry on comfort.

II:

The news I get at the clearing
isn't good: seventeen more
miles of fairly rough terrain,
then an island with no trees
and bears. Quietly, I'm given
a chance for more assured
survival—two   targets   are
hung   from   my   neck   and
shoulders.   Holding   the
bow   behind   my   head,   if
I   hit   both   marks   without
overshooting, I'll be gifted a
small boat   with rations; if I
miss, I'll be covered in honey–
fed leeches, let loose in cave
after   cave. At this angle, it's
hard to find the quiver   and
string. My anchor points have
shifted. I get only two shots. The
arrow in my stomach is pulled
at rough intervals of every
three, every five, every thirteen
seconds.   I take my time
deciphering the pattern.   Wait
for the break and   slack of the
rope.   When I feel I have it, I
extend my reach.

III:

When I arrive at the beach I
am full of infection. The sores
around the arrows in my
neck, shoulders and stomach
have given to seeping, and the
birds of the island caw hard
for their taste. By the water
line, as promised, is a kayak
and oars; there is also a crate
on a pallet. My throat is
dry and I urinate as I
walk. Removing the crate's lid,
I find worn cornered bricks, a
note and some soda. Bending
to drink, my mouth flowers
with parsley. I feel the roots
pick at my cheeks, my larynx,
choking my breath as I drool
down the dirt. When it stops, I
grab hold of the herbs and pull
gently away. Folded in
quarters, the note says I get only
one trip and everything must
go. For the kayak, the bricks are
too heavy. As we sink through
dark water, the beetles asleep
on my gums start to bicker.

IV:

Long plastic tubing sings
from my nose to the
surface. Holding my left
hand over my mouth, I focus
on breathing and rowing
with the right. Sunk to the
bottom, I tangle in
underbrush. Other wreckage,
shells, shadows surround
me. When the harpoons
come, I pick up the
pace. The arrow in my
stomach points to land
leagues away. Crabs pinch
and crawl in my ear for new
home. How to eat under–
water isn't the problem. My
hair is wet spins of dried
peanuts and okra. The water
is flat. *My captain,* I wail
through my hand to the
current, *this is just beginning.*

V:

Reeled into land, my arrows
are removed. The bricks are
unloaded in nice even rows,
and sitting on the dock are
young   women   with
babies. Men wearing masks
bring two trays of coffee. I
am   thanked   for   my
cooperation, told never to
mention these events to the
paper. As a parting gift, I am
asked to have their women. I
explain   my   body   has
hemorrhaged; I spill and leak
fluids of dark reds and taupe,
and my back has been nested
by hills of black ants. There
is laughter, and hitting, and
removal of clothes. I lie in
the shade of a beached
clipper ship. The women
form lines. A man in a hat
distracts all their children.

VI:

At a gas station I plead for a
ride to the city. I am wearing
no shirt and my nipples drool
pus from lightly indented
bite marks. There is quiet
murmur and looks of
concern. The lady behind the
counter hands me a napkin,
points to a bathroom then the
tail I have sprung. When I
come back from cleaning,
they show me pictures of
rubble–thrown streets. While
they tell me what happened, I
chase my tail through a
display case of motor oil. No
buses will run until
morning. In the meantime
I'm fitted with horseshoes—
put in a house surrounded by
crystal, branded a sign I can't
read by the light.

VII:

Kneeling and spitting I try to
water my lawn. The metal,
the rock, the loose bone and
cracked plastic have sanded
the grass a light brown to the
roots. My house is a pile of
sticks—the glass from the
windows looted for pillow
stuffing, the lid of my
mailbox held open with
bills. As I sift through the
fallout my muscles sink in;
my torso sags weak to pulled
skin on a frame, and heavy I
move surveying the scene: a
dishrag, bald tires, long legs
of my wife. I take her shoes
and walk back to the
street. The sky is pale gray in
the face of new evening. A
streetlight, erect, turns on by
a timer. I climb the wood
pole, hang from the crossbar,
weave and knot as I build my
cocoon. Once inside, I look
to the east and see dry
burning towns of industrial
business. Yelling for
employment, I make all
away the sparrows.

Principle Misstep:

In the alley, by the rear
entrance to an Italian rest–
aurant, a pack of wild dogs wrestles
me for the scraps.   Very quickly

they sense their advantage: they
secure the meat, corner the cheese–
es, pile the shrimp tails but leave
me the sauce.   I pocket some

bread half smothered in motor
oil, but that too is lost
in the fray.   While the dogs eat,
I throw forks at my ankles.   Although

we are tired, more rustling at the
door brings all ears to perk.   A woman
walks out holding big pans still
steaming.   Like the others, I look up

and whimper.   I am already on my
haunches when she bends and pours
hot grease down the length of my
bare chest and forearms.   The skin that stays

whole breaks out almost
immediately.   In the headlights of
a food service truck, I bathe the misfortune.

Bound. Down My Feet. My. Arms:
(Morphine Drip)

I:

Bound. Down my feet. My. Arms   carried. Stone. Carried   weight
I. Walked   until. I was   walked. Out– side. The   heat. Shook
trees. Lit. Water   my   far. My children.   Would. Know
no.   Settle I   stayed.   Talking the   night   canyon
its. Beckon   grown praise.

II:

And they. Found me   heavy. Low   earth   beat. Covered. My
over. Heard calls   I. Still. Waited poor   swallow. The   growth
no.   Leave the. Let not. Given to   me   I.   Raised a. Nation of   rags
planted rough   sisters. A   seed to grow   night. My.   Chest
shaved. Bare in   fashion of.   Times   the fields   threw. Up their
stalks their.   Stalks laid   stories   pricked.   Hands of   nothing
the. Way they moaned   all   one was   fever.

III:

Then ours. Then us. Then we dressed back. Our backs. Split days fields. Fell hard the. Song sung. Up to. Dry. Voices heard. Nothing wrong loaded our. Sons such. Cities lit palms came *bloodflieslocusts.* Handed my hand. Held calmly handed. Hand to bread. To water we spent. All. Night in. Our stomachs laid. Armies swelled charging they. Followed sad band of these bodies were born without work.

Manoleria:

My left wrist is tied to a bumper. My right, to a horse drinking water. The car and the animal face opposite directions. There are two women with flags raised high in the night. The engine revs and the horse is mounted by a jockey. Counting down from ten, the girls heavy their breath. The moon is hidden by lights from a city. When we start to pull away, even I am excited.

Combine As Assets:

It is hot in the office
of my loan officer. The
power is out. The windows,
painted over. I sweat and I
breathe in the chair
across from his computer and

after a time he looks up
disappointed. Around his neck
a tie has been removed. The top
three buttons of his oxford
are undone, and hair is pushing
small holes in his

undershirt. Dabbing his forehead
with an envelope, he lays out
an assessment of figures. Before
he makes to explain it, I reach
in my pocket for a handful
of teeth. I put them on

the desk next to his paper, and we
sit for a while growing hungry
of sleep. He says, finally, that my
business model is shaky; there's
little the bank can do
for me at this time, but to keep

them in mind for any future
financial needs. Pointing
to the teeth with my index, I
tell him it's okay. As we rise
to shake hands, his shirt
holds wet against the chair–back. Near–

ing the door, I pause to show him the wealth
of my pocket, how it goes down long
to a basin of jaws and how some
of the teeth have solid gold
fillings. *In this heat,* he says,
it must be hard to walk with that
weight. I hadn't noticed, I tell him.

Insufficient Funds:

The numbers on the keypad are worn
through to gray plastic. When I enter
the wrong security code three times in
succession, my card is ingested, and I'm
spit out a receipt of directions. As advised,
I take two large paces back, walk west
across the parking lot, advance into the
liquor store and await further instructions.

•

All day I pace through the
aisles. I am constantly asked if there is
anything I'm looking for, and at ten
minutes to three the manager talks to me
about loitering. I show him the receipt
and he points to a door and a stairwell.

•

Without light, the slope down is deceiving. There doesn't feel to be a railing so I focus my weight as I step and descend. By the time I get to the second landing, it's clear I am walking on horses.

•

With each step, they bray and
whinny and the ones without muzzles
drop their bits to the tread. I fall a few
times until I find the rhythm in their
spacing. When I reach the bottom, I'm
approached by a farmer in stirrups who
fastens me blinders while clubbing
my stomach.

•

Quietly, I'm dressed in a saddle and
ridden for hours around a circle of
oats. When I ask for water, I'm kicked
in the ribs and led to a utility closet where
pasteurized milk is kept in a box with fiberglass
jewelers' saws. As we tether to a drain pipe,
the farmer brushes my hair with a handful
of baking soda. Petting my neck, I'm told I
won't feel a thing.

Manoleria:

I walk to my mark and am handed a script. As I read aloud, I see my character is trapped in a mineshaft. For authenticity, the director reveals a wooden box with a ladder on its side which I climb into immediately. They give me a wireless microphone, an ear- piece, and ask me to begin Act One of Scene Two. With the lid closed, it's hard to find my lines. After a while the heat starts getting to me; it becomes more difficult to take full breaths and the rest of the cast complains when I miss my cues. The box is then sealed with Saran Wrap. I am reminded to be conscious of air supply. I'd say something back, but I'm already worried.

Trimming The Fat:

There is a knock at
the door. Rising from
bed, I adjust my night–
cap, light a tall candle,
and walk down the stairs.
Through the small parlor
window, I see a group of men
on horses waiting in my lawn—

hoods pricked high against
the spending dark, pitchforks
prodding the fresh sodded
ground. Having put on my
jacket, I step onto the porch
and join in conversation
over how this can go. The first
option is to fight. There would be

struggle. Torn clothes. Bricks
to my teeth, my forehead, my chin, but
also (they promise) a chance at recovery.
The second option is running. This would
involve fatigue. Sleeping in
barns. Eating what meat I could
find on the highway, and being caught
days, months, years from now,

mouth zip–tied to the exhaust pipe
of an abandoned minivan. The third option
I accept without thinking through. Using a
ladder they find in the shed, I climb to the
roof and lean against the weathervane. As I
steady myself, the men below move
into formation: shoulder to shoulder, six
standing per row. When I'm ready, they

raise up their prongs. There is a rope
tied around my waist. Before they pull back,
I take off my jacket.

One Stone, Three Birds:

Because   crowd loss. Because
empty. Because we   heard it
working three   counties
away. Because   investors. Because
marketing   plans. Because   print ads,
interviews, because   lights of all
colors. Because   murmur. Because
talk. Because   lines around
corners, because   tickets sell
out. Because   waiting. Because no
time for   practice. Because   opening
night crates   arrive from the   jungle. Because
chair. Because   whip. Because   tied to
the chair, because   smothered with
meat. Because   I wear the
mustache and   tall leather boots. Because
nobody   screams. Because   children with
smiles they   let out the lions.

Available Resource:

When the clapping dies
down, I step up to the mic–

rophone. Because of the
lighting, it's hard to see

the crowd, but most (I assume)
are hoping for a mishap. With

the help of my assistant, I go on
to explain the act. We show

the wooden wheel, the locks,
dispel any thought of an emergency

brake. As the stagehand calls
for volunteers, I begin dressing

down: remove my cape and
trousers, place my glasses

and fake beard on a stand. Once
I'm strapped in, the wheel is

spun counterclockwise. Someone
in a pashmina inspects the rounds

of a shotgun. Handed my apple, I
feel the chosen woman heavy her

barrel against my ever–birthing
chest.

Manoleria:

I am in a boat. I am wearing red socks, goggles, a necklace of lumbricid earth–worms. Most are dead, but one pulls soft at my beard line. As we move out to sea, I am offered a box of small crackers. Eating quietly, I watch while my ankles are hooked to lead weights with sturdy linked chains covered in cement. The air feels weak on my fresh shaven back. Handing me a nose–plug, they tie my wrists to the port bow with hair. My mouth is taped over and I make to shut my eyes. Before I'm thrown to the water, they ask I stay up as long as I can.

I Wait, There Is Chatter:

Two crewmen open the trunk
lid when I muffle the need
for a toilet. They allow me to
stretch, but keep a close eye
on the clock by the porthole. I am
shown to the bathroom and
stripped of my belt and shoe–
laces. Once inside, I spend
my time in front of the mirror. My
cheeks are swollen. My left
ear, covered with gauze. Where
they waxed my chest I am still
partly inflamed, but the map
carved into my breastplate has
healed surprisingly well: a circle,
seven perforated lines, six Xs and
a triangle. No matter how I stand, I
can't read the key tattooed on my
neck. Looking down, my ribs rinse
in the wake of some terrible
fortune. When I hear knocking, I turn
on the faucet. The gas rising up smells
of sweet leather gloves in my windpipe. If I
come out quietly, there's great promise of
water. I hold out for a radio.

Deep Pockets, Deep Pockets:

Leaning against a glass
door in the frozen
food aisle, I watch
my left thigh shake
wildly still. For

a moment there is
quiet, then the sound
of animal–feed
trailing the length of
my inseam: loose corn, old

cabbage, intestines, molars,
bushels of long grain
rye. In all directions,
the linoleum covers. A colon
lodges under the two

free–spinning casters, and
it becomes incredibly difficult
to push my cart. Embarrassed,
I slide back my right
foot and with a free

hand open the first door
behind me. Removing the
thin wire shelving, I
clear away bagels—I hold
cold cans of juice stacked high

in my lap and throw out the
omelets no fuss but the
noise. If I bend my
back. If I crane
my neck. If I twist my

leg upright to
stop the draining, I can fit
in the case without
energy loss. My breathing
whines in time with the

cooling fan. When
customers come to my section, I
hand them what we together
can stomach.

The Doctors Believed They. Were Out Of Rubber:
(Recovery)

The doctors believed they. Were out of rubber. Cement and. Would not sew my wounds on. Video. All day we were followed by. Cameras and. Children running with chickens. And. Pistols of teeth twice. Yesterday. You passed. Out while digging our sand. Filled latrine the. Colon I had was pushed. Back inside. Me behind. What was left of my. Liver. And kidneys next. To a box. Of automatic. Watches while we slept I. Talked through. Bad skin and. Cotton you changed my dressing and in the morning you changed. That dressing for a breast. Pump put it. With the others in. The neck of your camel was. Thirsty I had. Nothing held nothing where I could not keep food.

Audible Retraction:

In the hayloft of a neighbor's barn, I am just a torso. Propped up against the bailing doors, I stare at four limbs laid out before me: a child's arm, the leg of a rabbit, two twitching fins in varying stages of decay. Although I'm unsure, a letter I find indicates they'll work if I can somehow get them attached. Leaning forward, I throw back my weight in an attempt to lessen the blow. Using only my pectorals and chin, I rock my way across the plywood floor. Splinters in my chest sledge to keep me awake. Throughout the day, I hear horses below nicker while they're watered and fed. By nightfall, I've covered what I assume is eleven yards. This close, I see now the limbs are fitted with color–coded thread bolts. I'll sleep here. In the morning I'll call for help and when no one answers I'll hold with my mouth stale flesh in my teeth and screw in whatever's in reach.

Heyheyheyheyheyheyheyheyhey:

Because   weather. Because   dark
wind. Because   raft, because   sheet,
because   mast blown   part to the sea. Because
water. Because   weight. Because wav–
ing, because   waving, because   waving
my arms. Because   kicks. Pulls. Be–
cause black gone   blue, because   heavy
debris. Because   cold. Because
sand. Because   I will not   ever   get   off
of this island. Because   shaking. Because
vomit. Because   bark of large trees, be–
cause   digging a hole. Because   there is   no
way   to make   fire.   Because bugs in my
cuts I yell   out for new moon.

Deficit Ante:

Barefoot in thick, damp
grass, my ankles are
anchored to the ground with
lawn darts—rain is rolling

in from the west, and live
wires hang from metal poles
fastened to my back. To save
time, I initiate the bet, pointing

out to those listening who's
taking all the risk. From a half–
painted woodshed, a rotary
mower is removed. Before

it's started, the base is turned
sideways and a red push–tack is
set in the lip of its casing. As
the engine is primed, phone calls

are made. Soon, crowds settle
around me with blankets and ham
radios. When the draw–cord is
pulled, light smoke from the

housing kit scatters black
birds as it rises. Watching
the blade pick up speed, I
calculate how long I'll have

to reach in between cycles. There
is a heckler behind me loudly
singing *Little Woman
From Tokyo.* After I am fixed

with a blindfold, he quiets
down like everyone else. The children
holding sparklers are asked to
stand back.

What Must Be:

The window they've installed
in the center of my
back has made it hard to
lean forward. Although I've
been assured by many
different doctors, I'm concerned,
now, we elected the wrong
procedure. The oak frame
agreed upon has stretched my muscle–
mass shallow. The lip of the sill
keeps my jackets from
zipping, and where they used epoxy
my skin is infected—gray–black
scabs crack and puss through
the day, and at night it's suggested
I bathe in Neosporin. They test me
for wood rot, but the results are
inconclusive. For the next seven weeks
I've been advised to sleep on my stomach. Insurance
will cover the cost of a dehumidifier. They say
if I can keep the glass from fogging over,
they'll finally have their view.

Small There. The Screen Was. Out:
(Morphine Drip)

Small there. The screen was. Out its. Window cracked
glass. Still. Loading un. Loading. Unloading the. Light
to my. Body was. Swollen by. Water by rain at night my
mouth. Held. Open flat sticks long. Metal the. Base
of both. Cheeks cut. Rough. Splinters. I swallowed
I. Coughed through. My back. Stiff to a tree my. Feet
were. Bound. The fall came. In rhythms I. Never timed my
eyes closed when. Opened I. Was here. By the. Window
my. Plants not. Dry my lungs. Swished and shuddered their. Feed
like manure like we were to leave without sewing
me home.

Manoleria:

My tongue grows a rope,
grows a rope, becomes
chain. Lying in bed, I
pull at the links for over an
hour, periodically taking
short breaks for water. Once
I retch and heave acid, it is
clear I am close to a startling
discovery. Disappointed, I
stop when the sparks and the
peel move my liver—when
somewhere inside I hear
calling a shepherd.

Calm Market Scenario:

I am holding an ex–
acto knife, sitting
on butcher paper, no
pants to cover

my shaved right
thigh. With the first
incision, I attempt to
follow the general

gait of the betadine–
prep, but because of
the knuckles and drops
in the skin, I retreat more

naturally to the use of
my teeth. In a heat–
storm of veins, under
the carbonized glow of

exposed hypodermis, the
tissue of my rectus
femoris is studded with
50–watt metal–handled

light bulbs. The swelling
is moderate, but I worry
of rain and breakage. With
a dry microfiber dishrag, I begin

unscrewing, breathing long
hhhhaaaaas to keep away
moisture. There are nine
rows of eight bulbs and my wrist

very quickly gets pale
and sweaty. Once everything is
removed, I look in to see a
small community of handsomely

groomed dentists climbing out
of craters. I try to take pictures, but
there are too many shadows.

In Boxes Of. Hardened Egg Yolk We. Sat:
(Home Release)

In boxes of. Hardened egg yolk we. Sat. Guarding our. Luggage. You wore. The hat we. Bought. After your father. Died. I held a colon. Diseased from its. Root throughout the flight we. Talked through walls about sheets without. Bodies. When the turbulence came. There was clamor of. Weight of. Shifting of. Guessing to lean on. Our cardboard. Met open the. Cabin. Pressure was. High. Small sugar we. Cornered us into one noose you. Took from my. Hands a great cellar of waste.

Like Bricks, Like Bricks:

On a lighthouse ledge I stand
holding a boulder. Hugged
by a fishing net, the drag end
of the line is threaded through
a hole pricked wide in my
tongue. Last week, they
planted a cherry tree in my
abdomen. It's watered when
I sleep, and opening my
mouth I feel its dry branches
stretch the length of my
larynx. A pile of woodchips
helps to cover the roots
growing down through my
arches. From the tower, a
lamp and mirror spit–bright
the water every full eleven
seconds. I fear if I breathe
the stitching will
loosen. When I let go
the rock I move nothing
my body.

With Regret, They Make Moves To Sell My Kidney:

Because   I am leaving. Because
soon. Because   they find me   sleeping
by a window   in heat.   Because
parched. Dry.   Because   damp are my
pores caught   high in their   flash–
lights. Because   closer. Because
quiet   their march. Because   heels. Because
steps. Because   they've come with   rags of
blue   ether for   mouth.   Because one
moan. Because   jerk   still.   Because
wake. Because chest. Because   eyes,
open, roll   side–long to   white. Because
waiting. Because   must   make
certain. Because minutes,   hours,   now days sit
they next to   me with a   scalpel. Because
low. Because   many   short   breaths. Because there
is a buyer, small   money till   August. Because
I am   leaving.   Soon.   Because   here
in my building   the   hallways are feral. Because
deep   the   incision we   fall back the night.

Acknowledgments

Grateful acknowledgment is made to the editors of the following journals, in which some of these poems first appeared: *Forklift, Ohio; jubilat; Kenyon Review; Konundrum Engine Literary Review; 1913: A Journal of Forms; Ninth Letter; Sixth Finch;* and *Thermos.* Part of the poem "Went We. Inside. My Colon A Tree: *(Diagnosis)*" was included in the anthology *Disco Prairie Social Aid and Pleasure Club* (Factory Hollow Press, 2010).

Fellowships from the Fine Arts Work Center in Provincetown, the Iowa Writers' Workshop, and Augustana College were a great help in the creation/completion of this book.

Thank you to my friends, teachers, and family for your generosity and support. To Nam Le, Andy Stallings, Nick Dybek, Madeline McDonnell, Zach Savich, Vinnie Wilhelm, Michelle Taransky, Molly Minturn, Marc Rahe, Dora Malech, and Chicu Reddy—this book would not have been possible without your patient eyes and ears. I owe you all many, many things.

To Jim Galvin, Cole Swenson, and Dean Young.

To Amy Margolis.

To my parents, Nashi and Bobbi Khalastchi—אני אוהב אותכם. תודה.

To Jenny, Phil, Mia, and Zara.

To Caryl Pagel—"... adjusting, adjusting, according."

Photo by Phil Thomson

Born and raised in Iowa, Daniel Khalastchi is a first-generation Iraqi Jewish American. A graduate of the Iowa Writers' Workshop and a recent fellow at the Fine Arts Work Center in Provincetown, he is currently a Visiting Assistant Professor of English at Marquette University. He lives in Milwaukee where he is also the co-editor of Rescue Press.

Other books from Tupelo Press

This Lamentable City, Polina Barskova,
  edited and introduced by Ilya Kaminsky
This Nest, Swift Passerine, Dan Beachy–Quick
Cloisters, Kristin Bock
Stone Lyre: Poems of René Char,
  translated by Nancy Naomi Carlson
Poor–Mouth Jubilee, Michael Chitwood
Severance Songs, Joshua Corey
staring at the animal, John Cross
Psalm, Carol Ann Davis
The Flight Cage, Rebecca Dunham
Then, Something, Patricia Fargnoli
Calendars, Annie Finch
Other Fugitives & Other Strangers, Rigoberto González
Keep This Forever, Mark Halliday
The Us, Joan Houlihan
Red Summer, Amaud Jamaul Johnson
Dancing in Odessa, Ilya Kaminsky
Ardor, Karen An–hwei Lee
Dismal Rock, Davis McCombs
Biogeography, Sandra Meek
Flinch of Song, Jennifer Militello
Lucky Fish, Aimee Nezhukumatathil
The Beginning of the Fields, Angela Shaw
Selected Poems, 1970–2005, Floyd Skloot
The Forest of Sure Things, Megan Snyder–Camp
Human Nature, Gary Soto
Embryos & Idiots, Larissa Szporluk
the lake has no saint, Stacey Waite
Archicembalo, G. C. Waldrep
Dogged Hearts, Ellen Doré Watson
Narcissus, Cecilia Woloch
Monkey Lightning, Martha Zweig

See our complete backlist at www.tupelopress.org